HOW TO DO
THE GREASED
WOMBAT SLIDE

Poems by Pamela Miller

For information contact:
Unsolicited Press
Portland, Oregon
www.unsolicitedpress.com
orders@unsolicitedpress.com
619-354-8005

Cover Design: Kathryn Gerhardt
Editor: Summer Stewart

ISBN: 978-1-963115-99-4

This book is for Richard

and for Louise Miller, Bob and Kathy Chwedyk,
and Barbara Swift Brauer

POEMS

HOW TO ENDURE

HOW TO DO
THE GREASED
WOMBAT SLIDE

I live like so.
Heart as sail, ballast, rudder, bow.
　　　—Sandra Cisneros, "Loose Woman"

HOW TO DANCE

How to Do the Greased Wombat Slide

Ladies and gentlemen,
here's how the dance goes:

The acrobats come in through this door.
The zealots come in through that door.
A greased wombat slides down a pole
and everybody chases after him.

Desire sweeps in through this door.
The debutantes mince in through that door.
A greased wombat slides down a pole
and their skirts burst into flames.

The meek march in through this door.
The earth rolls in through that door.
A greased wombat slides down a pole
and proclaims himself Grand Usurper.

Our best selves waltz in through this door.
Our worst selves slink in through that door.
A greased wombat slides down a pole
and the whole game's up for grabs.

The four horsemen gallop through this door.
Armageddon thunders in through that door.
That goddamned wombat slides down the pole
and even you won't be able to stop him.

Ten Facts About the Author
That May or May Not Be True

for Nick Demske

1. On her opulent honeymoon in Bangkok,
   she repeatedly turned into a starfruit.

2. She has teeth inside her teeth inside her teeth.

3. Her code name is Good Golly Miss Anathema.

4. She is a tourmaline necklace.

5. Her poems are critiqued by flamingos.

6. She is allergic to anything.

7. She once attacked her mother with a headcheese.

8. She once stood glistening in the Sistine Chapel,
   naked as a golden egg.

9. She dreams of a man whose spectacular fingers
   will open her like a jewel box.

10. On the last night of her life, she'll be swept away
    by a tsunami of her own ingenious making.

My Husband the Science Fiction Writer
Tells Me About His Childhood

for Richard

I grew up facedown
in Chicago's spongy suburbs.
We ate dinner every night at the Heap O' Beef
and bought clothes at the House of Sad Plaid.
We vacationed down turnpikes bland as envelopes,
mailing ourselves off to some dank lake.

My mother switched on her minuscule TV
and watched nothing, nothing, nothing
for sixty years.

My dad was so cheap
he signed his name in blood,
too skinflint to invest in a pen.

My behemoth of a brother
"managed" my allowance,
snapping nickels in half and giving me neither.

So I hunkered in the attic like Quasimodo,
my defiant hair down to my knees,
reading *Famous Monsters of Filmland* magazine
and *The Tinfoil Hat Review*,

waiting for my rocket legs to sprout
and blast me into breathable air,
for my mind to stretch wide as a hovering spaceship
beaming me up to myself.

Pay No Attention

Mistranslated from Antonio Machado

Pale as a clavicle. Pale as a moan.
Vegetables, liver, and olives
stain the kitchen floor. Is it
my destiny to drink greasy brandy,
to wear my mother's obscene sombrero
exactly one year from tomorrow?
Oh, if only I could go to Dinosaur Camp!
Yes, I hear you. It's time to kill somebody.
Good old God said: "Blah blah blah.
O fie on your edited abandon, you poets!
O fie on your desperate pencils!"
It's as clear as the stars in the sea:
You've either got a truck or you haven't.
Pay no attention to Death in his inevitable galoshes.

The Burning Questions of Poetry

Who is Silvia? What is she?
Will you marry it, marry it, marry it?
Should I get married? Should I be good?
Shall I compare thee to a summer's day?
Do I dare to eat a peach?
Or does it explode?
Why should I let the toad *work* squat on my life?
When can I go into the supermarket and buy what I need with my
    good looks?
How much longer will I be able to inhabit the divine sepulcher?

Pure? What does it mean?
Does it stink like rotten meat?
O what can ail thee, Knight at arms?
Do I terrify?
Why does your brand sae drap wi' bluid,
Edward, Edward?
By thy long gray beard and glittering eye,
now wherefore stopp'st thou me?
Are you the new person drawn toward me?
Did he who made the Lamb make thee?

Fred, where is north?
Where are Elmer, Herman, Bert, Tom, and Charley?
"Is there anybody there?" said the Traveller.
Felix Randal the farrier, O he is dead then?
Márgarét, áre you gríeving?
Why should she give her bounty to the dead?
Why should we be organized to defend the kingdom of dullness?

21

What happens to a dream deferred?
What's the Greek name for Swine's Snout?
What are you thinking of? What thinking? What?
How can we know the dancer from the dance?
Is there no one who feels like a pair of pants?
Ramon Fernandez, tell me, if you know.
I walk through the long schoolroom questioning.

Autobiography Written in Disappearing Ink

Nobody ever called me Little Miss Wham-Bam-Boom
or Flamethrowin' Fifi or

anything, really. At school I was voted
Most Likely to Evaporate.

I seemed to be cloistered in a convent of skin.
I was colorless and quiet as a mollusk.

At thirty I got married
to a room full of dimly lit mist.

In the world's grand bouquet, I was a budbound rose
that blooms every fifty million years.

I wanted my life to be an opera, a conflagration,
not this tiny threadbare prayer mouthed by mutes.

When I die, I'll carve *Remember Me*
on a tombstone made of vanishing breath.

Poems from Three Sherwin-Williams Paint Colors

1. Bamboo Shoot

Six o'howling a.m. and we're
revving up our nerves' black gears
as we strompa, strompa, stromp through the mushy jungle
in our pixilated wingtip shoes
to shoot the sadistic bamboo
right in its corona of fangs,
our rickety bazookas just barely held together with goo.
The sun is a lichenous splotch on the sky
and the oldest of us is fifteen.
We're the doomed Pediatric Battalion
of Ankles, Ohio,
about to disappear into quicksand's shifty lips,
yawping a lugubrious battle cry,
our voices too vast for our heads.

2. Dard Hunter Green

The middle of gangly May and we're
belly crawling through the screeching forest's
corridors of sodden fronds,
our miniature jetpacks chirring,
our combat boots beribboned with earthworms,
to hunt the inexplicable dard
that spits noxious green gunk like a chlorophyll cobra.
But are we tremblers? Spiff spaff!
We're the mad-beard Commando Furiosos,

ornery as oak gall pie,
our Teflon chests relentless,
our rifles bristling with chutzpah,
oh we're Kali-armed pinwheels of destruction,
blasting Death's teeth out one by one.

3.   Belvedere Cream

London in the crevice of 1943 and we're
sidewinding like spirochetes down espionage's alleys,
an inch of blood asplosh in our brogans,
to cream that turncoat Belvedere,
that pianist of pain they call Hitler's Grater,
before he strangles us with poisoned gloves.
First we'll sizzle his molars till they pop!
Then we'll shove him in the avalanche machine!
But he slips through our flaccid grasp every time,
his fake skin crumbling in our hands.
We're the muck-it-up bungle-thumbs failure brigade,
useless like paint that's allergic to walls,
forever unbuttoning humiliation's blouse
beneath a sky full of snickering stars.

Mating Dance

You are a wizard with his hat between his legs.
I'm twenty-four vaginas baked in a pie.

I wear your embrace like a kimono of gold dust.
You're my antidote to questionable paladins.

You rearrange ghosts into doilies of lust.
I'm draped like a curtain over foreplay's window.

I careen through your dreams in souped-up glass slippers.
You're the murmurous frame around my heart's portrait.

You orchestrate our bodies' moist collusion.
I offer you the key to my hidden hieroglyphics.

I claw my way up terraces of moonlight,
I skate between the lines of anonymous love letters,
I waltz down the halls of the Orgasm Museum,
and who do I find but you, you, you!

Why I Don't Write Haiku

Make no little plans;
they have no magic to stir men's blood
—Daniel Burnham

why address the world
through the wrong end of
a bullhorn?

****

my poems don't want
to heave one dew-soaked sigh
then die like mayflies

****

want to watch poems
climb a half-inch Everest?
don't call me

****

make no teeny din—
let your poems rampage on stilts
like tornadoes

My Incandescent Past

Mistranslated from Pablo Neruda

I'm sitting here consuming a gargantuan pelican
while some vague cowboy pisses in the sink.
In the distance, refugees play their sober tubas.
The soloist rattles her coral castanets.

A package arrives from San Luis Obispo,
fragile as a crystal ace of spades.
Render unto Caesar his jealous jump ropes,
his unemployed llamas, the map of his calcified pout.

Once I had a river as sad as a hedgehog,
once I got married on the Day of the Dead,
once I had a sombrero of light
that filled the entire sky.

With a trace of champagne on my new fresh sleeve,
adore me as the sweetmeat that I am.

Sea Chantey

The sky is black as octopus ink
Oh no, sail me away
Seagulls shiver in robes of rain
Ready or not, we're all going to drown

The moon paints death's-heads on the waves
Oh no, sail me away
Hammerheads thread a path through the wake
Ready or not, we're all going to drown

The storm slips its brass knuckles on
Oh no, sail me away
Lightning struts on ghostly legs
Ready or not, we're all going to drown

Woe to he who argues with the sea
Oh no, sail me away
The mainmast snaps like a broken neck
Ready or not, we're all going to drown

The bubbles are few, the bubbles are small
Oh no, sail me away
And now there are no bubbles at all
Drowned, drowned, all of us drowned

Henry Fonda: An Erasure Biography

Henry Fonda's hat lulled his laurels. The stern actor discovered the Republic of Aristocratic Hands.

Fonda was a newspaper. Born grand, Henry attended the University of Becoming. The jobs he held included shooter, telephone, and the whole course of his life. He was persuaded to join the movement of well-known technical details. He expanded 150 sizes.

Fonda attacked General Tallulah Bankhead but the audience never appeared. He was signed for the role of a wayward fly. He reasoned with a long, hot bombshell. Exceedingly popular with office boys, Fonda refused wooden clothes.

Fonda is thick and blue. Among his "favorites": gardenia pudding and chocolate pictures. Favorite color: arguing. He is grateful to British wigs and his broken daughter and son. When the children grow up, they will destroy Rhode Island. Ten percent of Fonda is my darling.

Source text: Fonda's official 20th Century Fox studio biography, 1947

Ballet in Five Acts

I

O, the vehement whomp of evolution!
Suddenly our DNA
is twisting like Chubby Checker.

II

This is how I spend
my twinkle-toed nights: gluing sequins
on my heart while breakdancing.

III

Paranoia, in his
leotard of blood,
kicks up his sixty fierce legs.

IV

With each persnickety pirouette
the ballerina's skin
changes color.

V

Stop! This dance
is too intricate to do
unless you're dead.

What Poetry Is

It's an oddball
It's bioorganic
It's a prickly pear
It's a criminal conversation
It's an island of northwest Scotland, noted for its tweeds
It's April Fools' Day
It's a trampoline
It's an instrument for recording variations in tension
It's a shoot-'em-up
It's fortified wine
It's a soft, malleable, and highly toxic element
It's a third eye
It's Peck's bad boy
It's an arboretum
It's a temporary suspension of breathing
It's strong, stout, sturdy, tough, stalwart, and tenacious
It's an ejection seat
It's an embassy
It isn't what you think it is
It's in spite of everything

Makeovers by Fatima

Mistranslated from Nina Cassian

Your face is not appropriate for satori—
so impure, garish, maladroit.
Yet you too can soar like a svelte little cutie,
look young again in a patriotic obi,
and blissfully burn your old photos.

Why wear those awful ruglike pajamas,
that runny Rapunzel rouge?
I guarantee a chance to strut your stuff
in lingerie made of honey,
in a strapless ensemble of enigmatic microbes.

It's simply a matter of attitude:
You can live out your days as a frustrated frump
or blaze your stamp on the sun.
You're my perfect, perfect project.
Telephone Fatima today.

Trompe L'Oeil

I am not what I appear to be.
Does my blouse hide four red electric breasts
I can switch on one by one?
There's not an inch of me you can trust.

My molecules were bred to deceive you.
I'm a mannequin rolled in a carpet of lies,
my voice disguised in tangled anthems.
I am not what I appear to be.

Take a guess at what I'm made of.
Scrape off my face and you'll find . . . *what?*
If you unzip my skin, will I crystallize?
There's not an inch of me you can trust.

Affix your eye to my psyche's secret keyhole.
Are those spangles you see or are they spikes?
Like a coaxing doorway painted on a brick wall,
I am not what I appear to be.

You think you've sussed me out, but are you sure?
My legs collapse in prayer
but my arms are filaments of mischief.
There's not an inch of me you can trust.

I am not what I appear to be.
There's not an inch of me you can trust.
Just when you're convinced I'm the algebra of anguish,
my heart pops open like a bottle of spooked champagne
and joy shoots out everywhere.

HOW TO LOVE

Things I've Learned About Love

Don't try to tell me love is
blind. It has one glaring eye
smack in the middle like the Hand of Miriam.
Or, like the sense-defying stalk-eyed fly,
it puffs its transparent head full of air,
then pumps its eyes six feet out to the side,
a grotesque all-seeing capital T
always on the lookout for new suckers.

Don't tell me love is selfless.
I've seen it stomp and preen
and do the sage-grouse strut—
popping its floppy breast up and down,
whooping, "WE WANT WOMEN!"
and waggling its tail feathers
right in my face, clamoring for attention
like a bullfrog's *Ba-raaap! Ba-raaap!*

You don't have to tell me love
is strange. I know all about
its misfit menageries,
its *Vault of Horror* comic books,
the skivvies made of wriggling eels
it wears beneath its sailor suit.
Grandiose antlers don't impress me anymore.
When love dances on one leg
and bellows for its mate,
I've learned how to block its calls.

The Jealous Lover Puts On Her Makeup for Hell

*In an ancient Sumerian myth called "The Descent of Inanna," the
goddess Inanna gets dressed and puts on makeup
before going down to the underworld.*

Let darkest kohl outline
what's left of my pride.

If it's time to go to Hell
in a handbasket of nettles that I wove myself,
at least let me look the part.

If I must descend those blazing stairs alone,
bereaved of all the love I killed,
let my eyelids be painted with death's-head moths
to keep me company.

Let my cheekbones be gilded
with my alphabet of sins:
S for selfish, B for betrayer

but let my lips remain bare
as the rooms of my heart
so the flames' blistering kiss can brand them red.

Self-Portrait with Clip Art

At sixty-five I have forgotten how

to make my body eternal.

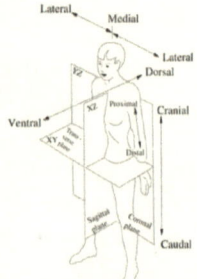

Most nights, I'm incessantly bisected

by phone calls from the unknown.

How much longer can I sit on life's mantel

without sliding off?

I'm still not ready to get up and dance

the Fighting Back Finality Tango.

What if I trundle to the end of the line

and there's nothing but air to meet me?

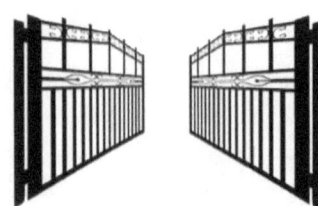

Or suppose I barrel through Heaven's front door

and plummet into the swamp?

Three Fates are two too many for me.

I prefer to travel alone.

Till Sir Nothingness arrives to dress me in dust,

I'll keep thundering out my name to God's sweet ears.

Naked on Easter Sunday

Mistranslated from Anna Akhmatova

Yes, it's unbecoming to primp one's own oxygen
but oh, my oblivious nerves!
Pablo, I laugh at your party hat,
your kleptocracy peeking through the eyes
of the not yet born.

Flocks of annoying pelicans,
four tons of crinoline from Ghana—
nix, no thanks, ptooey! I prefer Mexico
where I can soak my kneeknobs in the ocean.
That's where Alonso popped the question:

"Come home with me, nymph of Ohio!
Tomato of the anonymous moon,
elope with me and my famous bones."
I retorted: "Wait a minute, WAIT A MINUTE!
You're too toxic for my toboggan."

It's Easter and I'm naked.
Baryshnikov trembles in my palm.
Thank you, darling Balthazar,
for cranking up my push-pull heart.
I'm the cluster bomb who loves you like no other.

Love Letter to My Favorite Ghost

Poem made from movie lines spoken by
actor Laird Cregar, who died in 1944 at age 31

Mr. Samuel Laird Cregar
Eventide Section, Lot 37, Space 2
Forest Lawn Memorial Park

Dearest Haunter:

You're a pretty cocky fella.
You've had your own way for a long time.

Oh, I know your type. Your act is very charming.
A man can destroy what he hates and love what he destroys.

Allow me to be very frank with you:
Only the beauty remains.

Do you believe in hope?
"That's a horrible word. It's revolting!"

That's what *you* say. But you can't sell me on it.
Deep water is dark and restful and full of peace.

Don't you trust me?
Well, it's no use. I don't have to make bargains with you.

I'll follow you into your grave.
I'll write my name on your tombstone.

Someday you're going to talk in your sleep.
When that day comes, I want to be around.

What I Mean When I Talk About Poetry

for Jenene Ravesloot

I want to write poems that make mountains mambo,
that make synapses shimmer
like orchids grown in gold dust. I mean,

I want to write poems that scare even me,
that plumb depths of emotional sewage
Satan wouldn't stir with a ten-foot spoon. I mean,

Emily talked about taking the tops of heads off,
but I want to write poems
that roll hearts off the edge of the world. I mean,

I'm sick of all these poems
that read like walnuts with mayonnaise inside.
And by that I mean,

I want to write poems that are up to no damn good
but also rescue babies
from burning bassinets. You see,

what I mean is,
I don't want to write poems
that do nothing but wash life's windshield.

I mean, I want to write poems
that make Gaudí's towers swoon,
then claw the sky wide open.

Love Song Written After Viewing an Exhibit of Erotic Art by Women

With thanks to Woman Made Gallery, Chicago

Touch me in that place
where modesty melts,

where lust gapes deep
like a crack in the earth—

slippery sinkhole of desire,
raw as an oyster inside.

Kiss me in places
lips aren't supposed to go,

slurp secret sorbet from a quivering cup
no bistro would dare to serve.

Tonight let's leave our staid old love
waiting for the 10:30 bus

while we make porno movies
with a camera of Vaseline:

"Susie Polishes Peter's Golf Clubs,"
"The Longest Gun in the West,"

"The Night the Rains Came to Dusty Gulch,"
as a basementful of perverts yells "YEEEEEE-HA!"

Let me take you where our love
dances "Swan Lake" wearing nothing but a G-string:

I'm a woman, I'm an artist
and my canvas is the long, long night.

Ruthanne Replants Herself

I was bored with my click-clack factory job
stamping sunbursts on the heads of pins.
I was fed up with pleasing my husband
and his penis full of sludge.
I was sick of scrubbing floors
made of corned beef hash,
of spending my nights laying empty eggs,
squatting on a God-awful nest.

That's when I wrenched myself up by the roots.
     That's when I wriggled out of gravity's straps.
          That's when I grew my spider legs
               and galloped across the land.

          That's when I rolled out my own DNA
       like pulsating sheets of cookie dough,
    transfigured myself into a pinwheel of pistils
with a jones for being alone.

That's why I draw a red
line around my life
and wear it like a
wedding ring of spikes.
This is where I
replanted myself:
this invisible Eden where
nothing blooms but me.

Double Love Song, with Toads

Mistranslated from Georg Trakl

O, dear Arthur,
sleeping in your window of kindhearted guilt.
Dear questioner under the weeds.
Fill me with your warp-speed
suffering, dear squirmer.

O, dear Walter, dear liaison,
sinking in the brownness of August.
My auspicious Einstein with shaky hands.
Write me succulent poems full of
teenage instinct, dear purple-breasted señor.

O, the names of toads. The lassitude of beets.
All I desire from you two boys
is a lost night of laundered kisses.
Gild me with your vibrant branches!
Dear double lovers, gliding on a smattering of wings.

Going Out to Lunch with Emily Dickinson

Why am I not ready to meet her?
She's traveled such a long way to get here,
careening like a comet
down the turnpike of the dead.
Now she's waiting for me in the hallway
in her ragged flesh,
an unruly odor of lilacs rampaging through the house.
She speaks the way she wrote,
her phrases marbled with tremulous dashes.
"I know a Tearoom – slantways to the Stars – " she tells me.
Why am I so terrified of her?
Is it because her Big Bang poems
make mine look like scraps of snotty Kleenex?
Or that she might try to drag me back where she came from,
gripping my wrist so tightly my fingernails pop off?
"I-I-I-I still have some things to finish up,"
I splutter like a talking fish.
She just nods her translucent head,
patient as Whistler's mother.
"It was not Death, for I stood up,
And all the Dead, lie down – " she reminds me.

How Love Poems Get Written

for Richard, with thanks to
Faisal Mohyuddin's acrostic "Zinnias. How. Foreverness."

Remembering Mohyuddin's prayer rug of a poem
Into which the poet, squinting like Penelope,
Caressingly threads the names of his wife and son,
How daunting it is, my darling, to weave
Acrostics of love along the
River of your name, which suddenly
Descends into a snaggly thicket of

Coagulated consonants, and
How miraculous, then, to see
Wagon trains of frogs
Emerge by the hundreds from cabanas of mud to
Deliver these final lines like a thunderous singing telegram, as
You gallop to my side on a triceratops of bliss to
Keep my fingers steadfast on the loom.

Moving Day

When it's my day to die, I won't languish in bed
like the last drops of an evaporated ocean.
I'll still be a woman, dammit,
not a nightgown filled with sand.
Why should I merely vacate this body
when I can striptease it off, fling it away,
and do the ectoplasm squirm in some man's lap?

When my life's eviction notice arrives,
I'll take my mementos with me:
peonies big as beach balls,
buckets of sunset, mauve and gold,
that luxurious queen-size comforter
woven from my lovers' moans,
all my years of giddy whoop-de-doo
stacked neatly in boxes like heirlooms.

When my soul declares "Time for the next world,"
I'll race up the sky's rungs ten at a time,
but who'll be my new neighbors?
A pearlescent priest with seven penises of light?
A mile-high Mary Magdalene, demure in a robe of ice?
And what if God refuses to rent His mansions
to howler monkeys like me?
Aaaah, who gives a microbe's muff!
If Heaven's snooty doorman slams the gates in my face,
I'll just drift through eternity's back alleys
like a cloud of exuberant perfume.

Love Song Written on the Last Night of Summer

I don't know why the stars look so flimsy tonight.
Maybe it's that summer
is packing her bags for Antarctica,
leaving only a litter of blown-out roses,
her discarded costume jewelry,
while my fingers still dog paddle
the lake of your hair.
On this last threadbare night of the season,
every inch of air churning with cicadas,
the sun didn't set—it plummeted,
shattering like a pitcher of sangria
dropped on a concrete patio.
"I don't see us lasting past Christmas," you announce,
your voice a canoe gently breaking apart
as it glides me to the brink of the waterfall.
Tomorrow the leaves will start
choreographing their death dance.
Make love to me like an avalanche of embers
hurtling into a blizzard.

HOW TO ENDURE

Prayer to Four Gods, Because One Is No Longer Enough

Father of red skies and buttermilk,
Lady of skeletons and zeppelins,
Master of damage and drainage,
Holy Lord of whispers from shipwrecks,

Guide our ascent into corridors of comets.
Test our faith with dwindling miracles.
Make us kneel on needles in a hailstorm.
Smash our sins with implacable hammers.

Weave us wings to beat against the rafters.
Sharpen our teeth to gnaw away the bleakness.
Tempt us not into cavernous havoc.
Scour our doubt with Brillo pads of fire.

Hallowed be your hands that swaddle us in moonlight.
Blessed is your balm that numbs our sullen hungers.
Dreaded be your name, your shriek,
your poison on our pillows.
For yours is that glimmer of a kingdom
too pure for our uproarious souls.

Seeing Sweden the Hard Way

Mistranslated from Tomas Tranströmer

Into the blah hinterlands a-motoring we go.
I've got a never-ending pile of splattered socks I'm darning,
I've got half a skirt that's light on plot
and one single open-nippled bra.
We've got snacks made of telegenic sugar.

Our hasty French sedan hits a skunk and a naked man.
A truck full of sad potatoes keels over,
engulfing the mangy farmland.
My skull-shaped watch turns to dross in my hand.
"The devil!" you exclaim. "Cripes!"

Seven or eight fortune hunters have stolen our gold.
The stock market's falling. By midnight
all our blood will be gone.
Oh, to be back on the boat with our sassafras and whatnots!
Somehow some murky driver
has scraped all the words from our tongues.

Beauty at Sixty-Five

Cento from Anne Sexton

Once I was beautiful. Now I am myself
as I spill toward the stars in the empty years
with a singing in the head,
mouths calling mine, mine, mine.
Women are born twice.
I am beating all my wings.
I'm all one skin like a fish,
secretly naming each elegant sea.
A thousand doors ago
I thought I'd die—but here I am,
neither abstract nor pale,
a woman of some virtue and wild breasts.
Although I will inherit darkness,
good news, good news:
In celebration of the woman I am,
I soar in hostile air,
citizen and boss of my own body still,
so full of its immediate fever.

Invoking the Muse at Sixty-Five

Cento from Judith Johnson Sherwin

Come down from that clean room
     at the top of your head
Burst out of your four wits' brilliance
Be too loud for everyday wear:
     red swinging hair
     and arms of a flying carpet
Pull up with combs the wet chords roaring
Chew out the roots in windy ditches
Shake the bones out,
     white on white on white
Pick through these leavings,
     this reckoning from a disaster area
Grow into a questionable maturity
     beyond chart to measure the path
Lie out to stretch under your heat
Sing out the watch you keep,
     eyes unfocused, head turning continually
     under the snapping stars
Go rehearsing glorious laughter
     more resonant than alchemy
Come down to some feel of the poem
     stripped to one clear, unspeakable wail

Contemplating the Future at Sixty-Five

Cento from Amy Gerstler

Come winter, I'm due to wash into
that burgeoning unearthly glow
in all its voluptuous glory.
I plan to make a grand entrance
robed in clusters of bubbles,
a clamshell bodice, and tiny silver cobras.
Don't think I spend my nights brooding.
I know a thing or two about the path ahead
unfurling like an intricate cloud pattern.
Had my mother lived I could have taught her this:
When so much else has fallen away,
seeds disperse on the wind.
Sit down gently and ready your weapons for spring.
Whisper the following as the curtain descends:
A final fiery sip. OK. Time to go.

The Goddess Visits Me in a Dream
and Orders Me to Join the Resistance

She glides toward me on feet of smoke,
a bearded lady with a filigreed hairdo
but no head.

She stands beside my bed like a baobab tree,
waving her arms against a backdrop
of roiling sky.

She pummels my breasts to get my attention,
her insistent fists like clattering maracas
studded with stones.

She implants a miniature galleon in my spine,
then keelhauls the captain and drowns
the pleading crew.

I try to ask, "What do you want with me?"
but she flings my voice over the precipice
like a javelin.

She yells, "Poets are breaking evil's knees
but you're just planting portulaca!
Do your job!"

I snap awake
clutching lightning to my chest,
my armored legs striding, striding, striding.

This Poem Is Not for You

Mistranslated from Wisława Szymborska

Murmur, don't caterwaul. Waltz, don't whine.
Your mouth is too static to be a church window
and your pills can't be found in any proper druggie's dossier.
You can't get euthanasia from just any old oddball podiatrist
or by racing your dreary Stutz Bearcat
through the rickety gates of wishful thinking.
Why must you always protest Zeus' ruminations?
For crocodile's sake, stop dredging up
your convenient personal apocalypse.
I'm delighted to tell you for the last awful time,
you're wearing your two-piece penis all wrong.
Eat a beakful of botanicals, then get thee to Siberia.
This poem is not for you, my jazzless swain,
because it makes no easy sense.

The Spaghetti Squash Comes to Visit

We weren't ready for the squash when it knocked on the door with its head. The folks from the Visiting Produce Program had told us to expect it on Thursday, but our oblong yellow guest was four days early.

We hadn't had time to study up on spaghetti squash behavior. We assumed a vegetable visitor would be fairly sedentary, but it kept hopping around like an electric flea. It rocked back and forth on its legless butt. When we offered it a glass of water, it made a strange trombonelike sound.

Plus the goshdarn gourd only spoke French. *"La vie végétale, c'est une chose horrible,"* it sighed in its stringy, seed-filled voice. Mom thumbed frantically through her tattered old *Petit Larousse*, but the pages fell out in chunks.

The evening dragged on like the digits of pi. Eleven o'clock and still the squash wouldn't leave. It was watching TV, reclining on its side like some swollen, jaundiced football. We sat huddled together in pajamas of dread. Why had we agreed to host this thing? Who were we trying to impress? When the Schusters adopted a family of grapes, we didn't even send them a card.

We couldn't kick it out—that would be rude. We couldn't cook it—we'd go to jail. We lay rigid and wild-eyed in our beds all night, the squash singing howlingly till dawn.

Words to the Unwise

A stitch in time saves abandoned penguins.

The proof of the pudding is in Senegal.

No man is a membrane.

A bird in the hand is worth a can of spray-on pants.

When the going gets tough, the tough yell "FOGHORN!"

A fool and his money are timorous equations.

Early to bed and early to rise
makes a fish grow hair on its eyes.

He who laughs last lives forever.

How to Waste Time Looking Things Up on the Internet

How to tie a tie
How to make it in America
How to get a girl to like you
How to kiss
How to get pregnant
How to get out of a bad relationship
How to get out of the doghouse
How to get out of a car without showing your knickers

How to be happy
How to become a vampire
How to become a model
How to become anorexic
How to be a good girlfriend
How to become a police officer
How to beat Counterfeit Island on Poptropica

How to sew a button
How to sell weed
How to seduce a man
How to set up a blog
How to use chopsticks
How to use a tampon
How to use a bidet
How to use 911

How to tell a girl you like her
How to tell if a girl is a virgin
How to tell if someone is lying
How to tell your parents you're pregnant
How to tell if a diamond is real
How to tell if your Intel-based Mac has a 32-bit or 64-bit
  processor

How to do a bibliography
How to do a backflip
How to tell the difference between nerds and geeks
How to know the difference between love, infatuation, and lust
How to tell the difference between Japanese particles
How to tell the difference between cocaine and anthrax

How to meet cute boys
How to meet a man at forty
How to attract, seduce, and pick up women
How to meet new people without being creepy
How to meet broads
How to meet attractive, intelligent atheist women
How to meet and marry a billionaire
How to meet a celebrity
How to meet yourself (and find true happiness)

How to start a band
How to start a restaurant
How to start an essay
How to start a garden
How to start a movement
How to start triage
How to do things
How to make stuff

How to make great teachers
How to make the world a better place
How to make a difference in someone's life
How to get rid of your computer

Snapshots from My Nightmares

Headless people dancing.
Dead women golfing.

A drowned child stands on her hands.
A white monk and a black monk wrestle in a hurricane.

A shadow-faced specter serves Thanksgiving dinner,
the bird basted with ectoplasm.

A boy with no eyes
floats in a pool of melted butter.

My grandfather's ghost mows the lawn in tan pants.
A corpse reads the classified ads.

Pygmies with their teeth on fire
sink slowly into the swamp.

My dead father shakes me back to the past
and I swim away like a trout.

On Learning That One of My Books Was Found Among a Dead Poet's Possessions

I actually found [Pamela Miller's] book
among the belongings of a poet who had passed away
and his papers were chucked to the sidewalk
in cardboard boxes.

—Amazon customer review

Who were you, perished patron,
your shimmer too dim to be archived or inherited
instead of carted out to poetry's curb?
That stick-like old coot from the reading in Detroit
whose hand I had to crowbar from my knee?
A commando pilferer from small-town library stacks?
An emeritus prof who spent a snowbound afternoon
tunneling through the ant farm of my poems?
Once upon a time, you consumed this book;
oblivion spat it back out. When you died,
someone rummaged through your ashes
and found a piece of me, sparking like an ember.

A Few Small Clarifications

Silver-crested bird
soars from the flowering dogwood,
vanishes in moonlight

Actually, it isn't a bird. It's gleaming Athena in her burnished breastplate, busting out of Zeus' frontal lobe. Yes, there are definitely flowers, but they're Cadillac-pink petunias crowning the horns of a giraffe. And the moonlight comes from a frog-shaped jar in my pantry. At night I pour it into the waffle iron and nothing splendid dares to disappear.

This Much We Know

All disasters begin inside tiny padlocked boxes.
The periodic table is dissolving before our eyes.
Therefore, the Taj Mahal will become a hotel for ghosts.

All women secretly want to be Theodore Roosevelt.
But none would be caught dead in this centipede bikini.
Therefore, who am I to dip my fingers in boiling oil?

No cathedral of exhaustion has spires that point sideways.
An imploding neutron star can't dance on the head of a godsend.
Therefore, we must all till the futile fields of sleet.

All human beings compare themselves to battlefields.
All fallen warriors are reborn as shards of silence.
No man is an island, but some women are.
Consequently, our hearts turn so easily into ladders.
Therefore, the world politely refuses to end.

ACKNOWLEDGMENTS

Many thanks to the editors and publishers of the following magazines and anthologies in which poems in this book originally appeared (sometimes in earlier versions):

After Hours: "Ten Facts About the Author That May or May Not Be True," "Love Song Written After Viewing an Exhibit of Erotic Art by Women," "What I Mean When I Talk About Poetry," "What Poetry Is," "Pay No Attention" (as "Mistranslated Sonnet: Antonio Machado"), "The Jealous Lover Puts On Her Makeup for Hell," "My Incandescent Past" (as "Mistranslated Sonnet: Pablo Neruda"), "Seeing Sweden the Hard Way," "How to Do the Greased Wombat Slide," "Things I've Learned About Love," "Self-Portrait with Clip Art," "Ballet in Five Acts," "How Love Poems Get Written," "Going Out to Lunch with Emily Dickinson"

Blue Fifth Review: "Love Song Written on the Last Night of Summer"

Book of Matches: "Words to the Unwise"

Caravel: "Sea Chantey"

Circe's Lament: Anthology of Wild Women Poetry (Accents Publishing, 2016): "Ten Facts About the Author That May or May Not Be True"

Concho River Review: "The Burning Questions of Poetry"

Exact Change Only: "How to Waste Time Looking Things Up on the Internet"

Gyroscope Review: "Ruthanne Replants Herself," "On Learning That One of My Books Was Found Among a Dead Poet's Possessions"

MAYDAY: "Why I Don't Write Haiku"

Mojave River Review: "Henry Fonda: An Erasure Biography," "Moving Day"

New Poetry from the Midwest 2017 (New American Press, 2017): "This Much We Know"

Nixes Mate Review: "Naked on Easter Sunday," "Poems from Three Sherwin-Williams Paint Colors"

Olentangy Review: "Makeovers by Fatima," "This Much We Know," "Snapshots from My Nightmares"

Peacock Journal: "Double Love Song, with Toads," "Invoking the Muse at Sixty-Five," "Contemplating the Future at Sixty-Five"

Pirene's Fountain: "Beauty at Sixty-Five," "Autobiography Written in Disappearing Ink"

Poetry Super Highway: "Prayer to Four Gods, Because One Is No Longer Enough"

RHINO: "This Poem Is Not for You," "My Husband the Science Fiction Writer Tells Me About His Childhood"

Santa Clara Review: "The Goddess Visits Me in a Dream and Orders Me to Join the Resistance"

*82 Review: "A Few Small Clarifications"

The Disappointed Housewife: "Love Letter to My Favorite Ghost"

Third Wednesday: "Trompe L'Oeil"

About the Author

Pamela Miller has been gleefully embroidering the fringes of Chicago's poetry scene for more than 40 years. She is the author of five other books: *Fast Little Shoes* (Erie Street Press), *Mysterious Coleslaw* (Ridgeway Press), *Recipe for Disaster* and *Miss Unthinkable* (both from Mayapple Press), and *Mr. Mischief* (dancing girl press). Her poems have appeared in many journals, including *The Paris Review, RHINO, BlazeVOX, Otoliths, The MacGuffin, Nixes Mate Review, Wicked Alice,* and the late, great *Free Lunch,* and in the anthologies *New Poetry from the Midwest, How to Read a Poem, The Great American Poetry Show 2,* and *Circe's Lament: Anthology of Wild Women Poetry.* She has performed her work at readings in Chicago, New York, San Francisco, Detroit, and elsewhere. Ms. Miller has been nominated for the Pushcart Prize either five or six times (she's lost count). After a frenetic 36-year career slinging content for various public relations, marketing communications, editing, publishing, and freelance writing jobs, she now lives in blissful retirement with her husband, science fiction writer Richard Chwedyk.

About the Press

Unsolicited Press is based out of Portland, Oregon and focuses on the works of the unsung and underrepresented. As a womxn-owned, all-volunteer small publisher that doesn't worry about profits as much as championing exceptional literature, we have the privilege of partnering with authors skirting the fringes of the lit world. We've worked with emerging and award-winning authors such as Tara Stillions Whitehead, Heather Lang Cassera, Shann Ray, Amy Shimshon-Santo, Brook Bhagat, Kris Amos, and John W. Bateman.

Learn more at unsolicitedpress.com. Find us on twitter and instagram.

www.ingramcontent.com/pod-product-compliance
Lightning Source LLC
Chambersburg PA
CBHW031250120626
46545CB00007B/2749